SEASHORE

APRIL PULLEY SAYRE

TWENTY-FIRST CENTURY BOOKS

Brookfield, Connecticut

For my father's brothers and sisters—
those remarkable Pulleys

———

ACKNOWLEDGMENTS

Our thanks to the following scientists who reviewed portions of this manuscript: Derry Bennett, Executive Director of the American Littoral Society; Katharine Dixon, a researcher with the Duke University Study of Developed Shorelines; and Dr. Orrin Pilkey, James B. Duke Professor of Geology at Duke University.

———

Twenty-First Century Books
A Division of The Millbrook Press, Inc.
2 Old New Milford Road
Brookfield, Connecticut 06804

Library of Congress Cataloging-in-Publication Data
Sayre, April Pulley.
Seashore / April Pulley Sayre.—1st ed.
p. cm.—(Exploring earth's biomes)
Includes index.
Summary: Describes the physical characteristics of seashores, with a focus on North America, and discusses the various plants and animals that inhabit this biome as well as the effects of human use.
1. Seashore ecology—Juvenile literature. 2. Seashore—Juvenile literature. 3. Seashore ecology—North America—Juvenile literature. 4. Seashore—North America—Juvenile literature. [1. Seashore ecology. 2. Ecology.]
I Title. II. Series: Sayre, April Pulley. Exploring earth's biomes.
QH541.5S35S39 1996
574.5'2638—dc20
96-2420
CIP
AC

ISBN 0-8050-4085-4
First Edition—1996

Cover design by Betty Lew
Interior design by Kelly Soong

Photo credits appear on page 79.

CONTENTS

The water that makes up more than two-thirds of your body weight, that flows in your blood, that bathes your cells, and that you cry as tears, may once have flowed in a river. It may have floated as a cloud, fallen as a snowflake, bobbed in ocean waves, or been drunk by a dinosaur from an ancient lake. All this is possible because the water that's presently on earth has always been here—except for ice brought by comets hitting the earth's atmosphere. And all the water on earth is connected in a global cycle. This cycle is called the water cycle, or the hydrologic cycle.

Every day, all over the earth, water exists in and moves through this cycle. Ninety-seven percent of the earth's water is in the oceans. Two percent is in frozen glaciers and ice caps at the Poles. The remaining 1 percent is divided among the world's lakes, rivers, groundwater, soil moisture, and water vapor in the air. All this comes to a grand total of 326 million cubic miles (1,359 million cubic kilometers) of water. Every day, this water is exchanged among the oceans, streams, clouds, glaciers, lakes, wetlands, and even dew-covered leaves. Even now, it is being exhaled from your body, as moisture in your breath.

As the water cycles, at times it changes phase from solid to liquid to gas. The heat of the sun warms water on the land's surface, in lakes, in streams, in the ocean, even on the leaves of plants—and causes this water to evaporate, to turn into a gas. This gas rises into the air, cools, and condenses, eventually forming clouds and falling back to earth as liquid rain or solid snow or hail. This precipitation makes its way into streams, rivers, lakes, oceans, glaciers, and ice caps, and underground. And so the cycle continues. But it's not quite so simple. Each portion of the cycle is connected to others. For example, river water runs into oceans, stream water runs into lakes, and water from underground bubbles out of springs and into rivers. Water is constantly being exchanged among all the many places it resides on planet earth.

Almost anywhere water exists as a liquid, it is colonized by organisms—bacteria, amoebas, fungi, animals, or plants. Some watery habitats have particular physical conditions and particular kinds of plants and animals inhabiting them. These are aquatic biomes: ocean, river, lake, and coral reef. Where these aquatic biomes mingle with terrestrial, or land, biomes, they may form special, semiaquatic, fringe communities. Wetland and seashore are two of these communities that are unique enough and widespread enough to qualify as major biomes.

All aquatic and semiaquatic biomes—ocean, river, lake, coral reef, seashore, and wetland—are influenced by regional climate and the lands nearby. These biomes are also linked to one another, by ever-moving water molecules and the global water cycle through which they flow.

🐚 1 🐚
THE SEASHORE
BIOME

Every minute, every hour, every day, the border between land and sea changes. Tides rise, covering land, and fall, revealing it. Like a jackhammer, surf pounds at rock, sculpting caves and crumbling cliffs. Currents transport sand, building up some beaches and wearing away others. Over centuries and millennia, sea level rises and falls, making mountaintops into islands and then into mountains again. In the end, there's no definite border separating land from ocean—only a tug of war between the two. The site of this battle is the seashore, one of the most dynamic environments on earth.

Surprisingly, animals and plants thrive on this turbulent fringe between ocean and land. Limpets and barnacles stick to rocks. Crabs hide in crevices. Sea stars with hundreds of sucker feet clamp themselves securely to shore. Worms burrow in sand. Snails cling to limp, colorful seaweeds that grow glued to a rim of rock. And shorebirds skitter back and forth, plucking worms and crabs from the sand.

Like rain forest and desert, seashore is a biome—an area that has a certain kind of community of animals and plants. But unlike desert, tundra, and other terrestrial—land—biomes, seashore does not have a characteristic cli-

Shorebirds search for food where the land meets the sea.

mate. It occurs all over the earth where land and ocean meet, from cold Arctic coasts to hot tropical beaches. Some scientists consider seashore only an ecotone—a place where two other biomes mingle. But seashore is so extensive, and has so many characteristic plants and animals, that here we have considered it as a biome in its own right.

This book discusses two major types of seashore: sandy beach and rocky shore. Strictly speaking, however, seashore could also encompass mangrove swamp and salt marsh. But those two habitats have more features in common with other wetlands, so they are covered in the *Wetland* book of this series.

For millions of years, the seashore biome has been a meeting place for land organisms and ocean organisms. Today, in addition, it's an active human habitat. Coasts are the site of some of the earth's most populated cities, including Tokyo, Djakarta, Bombay, Rio de Janeiro, Los Angeles, and New York City. Every day, coastal populations grow rapidly, increasing environmental pressures on the seashore. Coping with these pressures will require careful planning and a deep understanding of the seashore biome.

TYPES

There are two major types of seashore:

- Rocky shore—characterized by rocky outcroppings and cliffs.
- Sandy beach—characterized by wide, flat expanses of shifting sand.

DIVISIONS

Seashores are divided into three main parts:

- A splash zone (also called the supralittoral zone)—this area is above the high-tide mark. Only salt spray or wave splash reaches it, so it's fairly dry.
- An intertidal zone (also called the littoral zone)—this area is between the high- and low-tide marks; it is dry at times and wet at other times.
- A subtidal zone (also called the sublittoral zone)—this area is beneath water, even at low tide.

PHYSICAL FEATURES

Seashores are:

- Exposed to saltwater waves and affected by ocean tides.
- Made of rock and sand of many colors and from many sources.
- Constantly changing. Rock and sand are eroded—worn away or carried away—from parts of the shore, and transported and deposited elsewhere along the shore.
- Frequently damaged by powerful storms, including hurricanes.
- Affected by sea level rise.

ANIMALS

- Animals are adapted to burrow in sand or hold tight to rock surfaces.
- Many animals have special features that help them survive drying out when they are exposed at low tide.
- Animal communities show a clear zonation along the shore. They grow in bands, according to how often they are reached by tides.
- More animals are found lower on the shore, and fewer are found in higher spots, where they are less often wetted by tides.
- Rocky shores have a moderate animal diversity, or number of animal species, compared to other biomes. Sandy shores have a low animal diversity.

PLANTS

- Seaweeds are common and grow in great variety on seashores, where sunlight is plentiful and surfaces for attachment are available.
- Waves and currents bring plankton—tiny, floating ocean plants—to the seashore.
- Tiny algae grow on rocks like frosting and in the spaces between sand grains.

❧ 2 ❧
NORTH AMERICAN
SEASHORES

There's much more to do on North American seashores than just get a tan. In Mexico, you can watch baby sea turtles stream across the shore to the sea. In Washington State, you can pick up a sea star and feel its sucker feet on your hand. In Maine, you can clamber over a seaweed-strewn shoreline, where fog closes in like a cloud. Or you can surf waves in southern California, kayak among killer whales in Alaska, or watch puffins swirl around Newfoundland cliffs. All this is possible on the mere fringes of a continent—North America's amazing seashore.

A startling seashore variety—wide sandy beaches, rocky cliffs, and pebbled shores—exists in North America because of its turbulent geologic history. Over thousands and millions of years, scouring glaciers, erupting volcanoes, rising and falling sea levels, and fierce storms have shaped the continent's coast. As a result, each region has its own particular shoreline features.

Northern Fjords The coasts of Alaska and northern Canada are filled with glacier-carved valleys. Thousands of years ago, when sea level rose, these valleys filled with seawater, forming fjords. In fjords, waves break against pebbled beaches and steep-walled cliffs where seabirds nest by the thousands. Both Canada and Alaska also have lower-lying coasts with tundra, sandy beach, and salt marsh. Newfoundland even has some cobble beaches covered with large, smooth, colorful rocks.

The Drowned Coast   Off the shore of New England, ancient forests, rivers, and valleys lie hidden beneath ocean waves. That's because the edge of the sea was once hundreds of miles farther seaward than it is today. About ten thousand years ago, as the last ice age ended, sea levels rose and the ocean began pushing gradually inland. New England's coast, often called the drowned coast, is made of cliffs that were once inland mountain ridges. This coastline is made up of jagged headlands—rocky cliffs on fingers of land that jut out into the ocean. In between these fingers, small, sandy "pocket" beaches form in coves from sand

The rugged coast of Maine features mostly rocky shores but also some sandy beaches.

worn away from the shore. Cape Cod is a pile of rubble dropped by a glacier when it melted and retreated at the end of the last ice age.

White Sands and Barrier Islands A few rocky spots remain along New York and Rhode Island, but most of the Atlantic Coast from New York to Florida is sandy beach backed by dunes. These beaches were built mostly by sediments from the numerous rivers that drain the Atlantic Coast. Sand from the rivers is also swept out to form the barrier islands that parallel the shore. These barrier islands protect coastal marshes, bays, and estuaries from the brunt of ocean waves. The Gulf Coast from Florida to Texas has similar sandy beaches and barrier islands. But the Gulf Coast is also shaped by the Mississippi River, which deposits a tremendous load of silt.

Fiery Coasts and Surfers' Paradise On the Pacific Coast, from Washington to central California, the land has been sculpted by volcanoes and earthquakes as well as ocean waves. In between rocky headlands lie long, straight beaches formed from eroded rock. Offshore, strange arches, domes, and caves are carved by waves that pound the shore's soft rock. Southern California has a high-energy shoreline buffeted by powerful waves. Wide sandy beaches and sandstone cliffs line this coast, which is also prone to earthquakes. Shifting sands, underwater cliffs, and islands make up a shoreline complex in its structure and geologic history.

NATIONAL SEASHORES
Five hundred miles (806 kilometers) of the 88,000-mile- (142,000-kilometer-) long coastline of the United States is protected by the government as National Seashore, a type

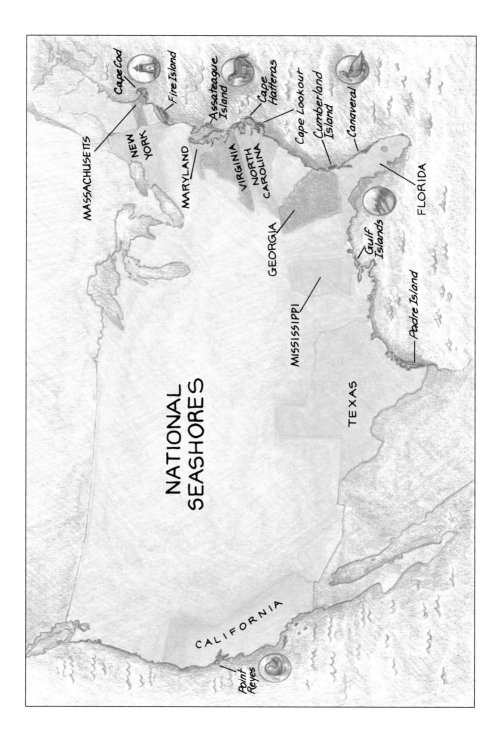

NATIONAL
SEASHORES

Point
Reyes

CALIFORNIA

TEXAS

Padre Island

Gulf
Islands

FLORIDA

MISSISSIPPI

GEORGIA

Cumberland
Island

Cape Lookout

Canaveral

NORTH
CAROLINA

VIRGINIA

Cape
Hatteras

Assateague
Island

MARYLAND

MASSACHUSETTS

NEW
YORK

Cape Cod

Fire Island

of coastal national park. These ten National Seashores encompass sandy beaches, rocky cliffs, and remote islands—a small sampling of North America's remarkable shores.

Cape Cod National Seashore, Massachusetts   As an artists' colony, the site of five lighthouses and numerous shipwrecks, and the spot where the Pilgrims first came ashore, Cape Cod has a rich human history. But this bent-arm-shaped peninsula has interesting natural features, too. Cape Cod formed from a pile of debris—a moraine—left by a retreating glacier. Today, it continues to change because of its shifting sand dunes and migrating beaches. Great Island, which was once a separate island, is now connected to Cape Cod.

Fire Island National Seashore, New York   An official federal "wilderness area" exists within 50 miles (80 kilometers) of Manhattan. This wilderness is part of Fire Island National Seashore, which preserves the natural areas of a narrow barrier island that contains many small communities with houses and shops. Behind the island's sandy beaches and dunes lies a hollow where a sunken forest of holly, sassafras, and tupelo trees grows. Many flock to this island—not just people, but also migrating ducks, geese, and monarch butterflies.

Assateague Island National Seashore, Maryland and Virginia   This barrier island contains freshwater marshes with sandy beaches. Each year it hosts thousands of migrating birds—ducks, geese, warblers, terns, sandpipers, and even peregrine falcons. The wild horses that roam Assateague and neighboring Chincoteague were the inspiration for the classic children's book *Misty of Chincoteague*, by Marguerite Henry.

Wild horses live on Assateague Island National Seashore.

Cape Hatteras, North Carolina   With 70 miles (113 kilometers) of sandy beaches lined with sand dunes, gnarled forests, and salt marshes, Cape Hatteras is a nature lover's paradise. It has a fascinating history, too: the famous Cape Hatteras lighthouse faces a region called the Graveyard of the Atlantic because it's riddled with the debris from more than six hundred shipwrecks. Raging storms, shifting underwater sand ridges, and maritime battles doomed these ships to sink.

Cape Lookout, North Carolina   Located southwest of Cape Hatteras, Cape Lookout contains Portsmouth Island, Core Banks, and Shackleford Banks. These three islands are part of the Outer Banks—the barrier islands protecting North Carolina. A small but wild seashore, Cape Lookout has sandy beaches and dunes with just a few houses. It's accessible only by ferry or private boat.

Cumberland Island National Seashore, Georgia   To get to this wild island, you have to make reservations to be among the few hundred people ferried daily to its shores. Beaches, sand dunes, live-oak forests, and saltwater marshes host a variety of wildlife from fiddler crabs to armadillos, a recent arrival. Ancient middens—piles of shells—mark the spots where Native Americans feasted on shellfish hundreds of years ago.

Canaveral National Seashore, Florida   Canaveral National Seashore and Merritt Island National Wildlife Refuge together form a wild buffer zone bordering Cape Canaveral and the Kennedy Space Center, where space shuttles are launched. The Canaveral National Seashore contains a sandy barrier island and freshwater marshes. It is home to 1,045 plant species, 310 bird species, and 22 endangered animal species, including nesting loggerhead turtles.

Gulf Islands National Seashore, Mississippi and Florida   "For want of grass the sand is lost; for want of sand, the dune is lost; for want of the dune, the island is lost; for want of the island, the harbor is lost," says a sign on West Ship Island in the Gulf Islands National Seashore. The reason is

Canaveral National Seashore and Merritt Island National Wildlife Refuge surround the Kennedy Space Center, the site of space shuttle launches.

that people used to collect sea oats from the dunes for flower arrangements. Without the roots of sea oats to help hold the sand, the dunes were blowing away. Now that collecting sea oats is illegal, dune destruction has slowed. But the islands continue to move naturally. Longshore currents are carrying the sands of these islands westward. Petit Bois Island, which in 1850 was shared by Mississippi and Alabama, is now entirely in Mississippi!

Padre Island National Seashore, Texas Padre Island is a barrier island with magnificent sand dunes and beaches; it borders the Laguna Madrea, a shallow, salty body of water. For ten years, biologists have been relocating the eggs of

Kemp's ridley sea turtles from Mexican beaches to Padre Island to reestablish a population of these endangered sea turtles.

Point Reyes National Seashore, California At Point Reyes, you can play with sea stars in tide pools, observe birds, or watch migrating gray whales pass along the shore. Pounding surf, riptides, and a strong undertow make swimming treacherous near the rocky beaches and crumbling cliffs. But swimming is possible off sandy beaches in several protected coves. The San Andreas Fault, where two continental plates meet, runs near the park headquarters. During the 1906 earthquake in San Francisco, the Point Reyes peninsula moved 16.4 feet (5 meters) to the northwest!

Sea otters crack open clams using rocks as tools.

National Seashores provide protected places where people can enjoy beaches in their natural state. National Seashores are also critical to other beach visitors: the feathered, furred, scaled, and shell-covered kinds. Horseshoe crabs by the hundreds climb up Carolina beaches in spring to lay pale green eggs. Sea otters float on their backs, cracking clams on their bellies, not far off California shores. And endangered piping plovers guard Atlantic beaches where their sand-colored eggs are laid.

❀ 3 ❀
PHYSICAL FEATURES
OF SEASHORES

Every day, the surface of the ocean is in motion. Currents, like giant rivers, flow for thousands of miles. Waves splash against seashores. Tides rise and fall. All these forces impact the seashore, changing it in complex ways.

THE OCEAN IN MOTION

As surfers know, every wave is different. A wave can be a few inches high or up to 112 feet (34.1 meters) tall. In general, wind causes waves, but on rare occasions, earthquakes and underwater landslides cause waves, too. A wave's size and power depends on how far, how fast, and how long the wind blows across the water's surface. An ocean wave, like a light wave or a sound wave, is not traveling water at all, but traveling energy. As a wave passes by, water molecules move upward and forward, then circle back to their original position. Water molecules don't travel far horizontally; only the energy does. When waves approach shallows near shore, the deeper water is slowed by friction from contact with the ocean bottom. But water on the surface is still moving quickly, so it starts getting "ahead" of the water below. It moves forward, forming a crest, then spills over as the wave breaks.

Current Events If you swim straight out from the shore, tread water for ten minutes, then swim straight back to shore, you'll probably find yourself downshore from where you started. A longshore current carried you there. A current is very much like a river that flows within the ocean. Unlike a wave, a current moves water in large amounts, often over large distances. For instance, a current called the Gulf Stream carries warm water from the Gulf of Mexico north along the Atlantic Coast of the United States and then east toward Europe. What causes most currents? Strong winds, such as trade winds and westerlies, blow for a long time over long distances, pushing the water along. But a special kind of current called a longshore current is created by waves crashing against the shore. Longshore currents travel parallel to the shore, sweeping swimmers far from where they entered the water.

Let 'Er Rip! When you're swimming near shore, you may feel a current deep in the water, pulling you out to sea. This is the undertow, or backwash current. When waves hit the shore, some of their power is bounced back underwater, in the backwash current. This current does not go very far. But on steeply sloped beaches it can be strong. (If you get caught in a backwash current, you can swim toward shore or wait until the current weakens, so the waves can push you in to shore.) A much stronger, more dangerous current is a rip current, sometimes called a riptide. Rip currents occur when currents pushing toward shore are deflected away from land through a narrow channel or a gap between two sandbars. These currents can push you out to sea. But rip currents are usually narrow, so if you get caught in one, simply swim parallel to the shore to escape it. Whatever you do, don't panic. Swimmers can safely escape rip currents.

THE RISE AND FALL OF TIDES

You pick a spot on the beach, set out your towel, and go for a nice long walk. But when you return, your towel is floating away! The tide has risen while you were gone. Shorelines all over the world experience tides, a periodic rising and falling of the water level. Even lakes have tides, although they are not as noticeable as ocean tides.

Highs and Lows   Along most of North America's Atlantic Coast, water levels rise 2 to 10 feet (0.6 to 3 meters) between low tide, the lowest water level of the day, and high tide, the highest level. In the Mediterranean, there may only be a few centimeters difference between low and high tide each day, but in the Bay of Fundy, in Nova Scotia, the tide rises a whopping 43 feet (13 meters) from low tide to high! The slope of the seashore affects how far tides push inland or recede. On a steep, rocky cliff, a one-foot change in tide uncovers a one-foot strip of cliff. But a one-foot change in tide can uncover a broad beach if it's very gently sloped. When the tide is out near Mont-Saint-Michel, France, it's really

These photographs show the dramatic difference between high tide (left) and low tide (right) at the Bay of Fundy.

out—as much as 9 miles (14.5 kilometers) away! In such places, tides can whoosh in quickly, advancing so fast you can't outrun them. People caught unaware, out on mudflats, can drown when such tides advance.

Tide Types   There are three main types of tides: semidiurnal, diurnal, and mixed. Areas affected by semidiurnal tides, which are felt along North America's Atlantic Coast, have two low tides of similar height and two high tides of similar height every 24 hours and 50 minutes. California experiences mixed tides: two high tides of different heights and two low tides of different heights every 24 hours and 50 minutes. Pensacola, Florida, has diurnal tides: only one low tide and one high tide per 24 hours and 50 minutes.

The Reason for Tides   Tides are caused primarily by the gravitational pull of the moon on the earth's oceans. As the moon orbits the earth, it pulls on the ocean, creating a bulge of ocean water that follows the moon around the earth. At the same time, a bulge of water spins out on the opposite side of the earth because of other forces. Additional factors, including the gravitational pull of the sun and the position of the continents, affect tides, too. So from day to day and place to place, tides vary in height, timing, and how far inland they reach.

Super Highs and Super Lows   Every fourteen days, during the new moon and full moon, the gravitational pull of the sun and moon are combined in one direction. As a result, part of the earth experiences particularly extreme tides, called spring tides. (Spring tides are so named because the water "springs up," not because of season.) During spring tides, high tides are very high and low tides are

· YOUR LIFE, THE MOON, AND THE TIDES ·

Every day, probably without your knowing it, the sun and moon exert a pull on you. It's the same pull that makes the oceans bulge outward, creating tides. It makes the atmosphere pouch out several miles into space. It even makes the earth's continents rise and fall several inches daily. This powerful force is based on attraction.

Everything in the universe that has mass is attracted to everything else that has mass. We call this attraction gravitation. On earth, a ball thrown in the air falls downward because of the earth's gravitational attraction for the ball. The moon and sun also have a gravitational attraction for the earth and objects on the earth. It's just not very noticeable because they are so far away. However, their gravitational attraction *is* noticeable on something as big as the ocean. The sun and the moon pull the earth's oceans toward them, making it bulge.

The moon, which is much closer than the sun, has the most gravitational pull on the earth's oceans, so the bulge is closest to the moon. This bulge travels each day as the moon orbits the earth. But it's not quite so simple. The moon's orbit, the earth's orbit around the sun, and the earth's revolution all affect the position, timing, and size of this bulge. To make matters even more complex, there's another force at work, warping the earth's oceans—centrifugal force. Centrifugal force creates a bulge of raised water on the side roughly opposite to the bulge caused by the moon.

Gravitation and centrifugal force affect the tides. And they affect you, too. The pull on your body is so strong that you actually weigh less at the time of high tide than you do at the time of low tide!

very low. Every fourteen days, during the quarter or three-quarters moon, neap tides occur. At that time, the sun and the moon are pulling the earth's water in different directions, so they partly cancel each other's pull. That creates a lower high tide and higher low tide—a smaller range of tidal movement than usual.

SAND AND SEA

Sand isn't a particular kind of rock, but rather a size. Any rock 0.002 to 0.079 inch (0.05 to 2 millimeters) in size is called sand. Beach sand can come from many different sources. New England's beach sand is made of quartz, feldspar, and other hard rocks. Bermuda's pink sand beaches are made of limestone, coral, and shells. Hawaii's black sand beaches are made of volcanic rock. Some tropi-

The rough, pitted surface of a sand grain is revealed by this photograph, taken through a scanning electron microscope.

SEE THE SALT

Put a teaspoon of salt in a cup of water. (Or put 35 grams of salt in a liter of water.) That's about how salty ocean water is. It's 35 ppt, parts per thousand, meaning there are 35 pounds of salt for every 1,000 pounds of water. But the ocean contains more than sodium chloride, or table salt. It also contains salts of magnesium, sulfate, potassium, calcium, and other elements. To see sea salt, fill a pan with a shallow layer of ocean water and set it out where it won't be disturbed. In a few days, the water will evaporate. The white crust left behind is sea salt. This same technique, on a bigger scale, is used to harvest salt from the ocean. Ocean water is trapped in shallow basins and allowed to evaporate, and then the salt is collected.

cal sands are made with the help of parrotfish: these strong-jawed fish chew up and swallow coral to get the algae that live inside. Once the coral comes out the parrotfish's other end, it's in small, sand-size particles!

SEASHORES ON THE MOVE

If you drive along the California coast, you'll see plenty of evidence that seashores change. In Santa Cruz, part of Cliff Drive has fallen off a cliff. Shoreline Drive in Buena Vista has long since washed away. In one town, Fourth Street has an ocean-front view because First, Second, and Third Streets have eroded!

Constant Change Coasts change every minute of every day, from season to season and from year to year. Ocean waves hammer rocky coasts, causing hillsides to slump and pummeling boulders into sand. Currents carry this sand to quiet coves, forming pocket beaches along the shore. Sandy beaches grow narrow in winter as storms carry sand offshore to form sandbars. Then summer waves bring the beach sand back, to form a broad, summertime beach. Wind also plays a role, blowing sand from beaches to dunes or from dunes out onto beaches. And all year long, longshore currents carry sand from one beach to another along the coast. Constantly in flux, some beaches grow wider or longer; others shrink. (In South Carolina, Morris Island has retreated, leaving its lighthouse 1,200 feet [365 meters] offshore!) Most of all, beaches move, gaining sand in some places and losing it in others, and shifting their position along the coast.

Climate Change and Sea Level Rise   For the last three thousand years, sea level has stayed fairly stable, with only a few ups and downs. But in the last one hundred years or so, sea level has risen as the earth has warmed. When the earth's climate warms, sea level rises for two reasons. First, the heated ocean expands, taking up more space. And second, the polar ice caps melt, adding water to the ocean. Along the Atlantic and Gulf Coasts of the United States, sea level has been rising at a rate of about 1 foot (30 centimeters) per century. That may not sound like much, but it's enough to begin flooding low-lying areas such as Houston, Texas, and parts of Louisiana. Even a small rise in sea level can flood a large coastal area if it is very flat or only gently sloped.

Migrating Beaches and Rolling Islands   As sea level rises, beaches tend to move gradually inland. But these days, the inland migration of many beaches, marshes, and mangrove swamps is blocked by human developments and paved-over land. Nevertheless, the force of storm waves and hurricanes can force beaches and islands to move. Barrier islands, which are sand islands parallel to the shore, have been rolling toward the Atlantic Coast for thousands of years! How does this happen? Higher seas create storm waves that wash over the islands and pour through inlets, carrying sand to the side nearest the mainland. This causes the island to roll over itself and actually move toward the mainland. Usually, the islands don't smack into the mainland because as sea level rises, it floods even more of the low-lying edge of the mainland.

The Pollution Connection   Sea level rise occurs naturally, but people can affect it, too. Many scientists feel that the warming of the global climate is linked to air pollution from automobiles, lawn mowers, backyard grills, fireplaces, industry, the burning of tropical forests, cattle ranching, and other activities. Gases from these activities rise up into the atmosphere, joining and thickening a gas layer that already exists. This layer lets in ultraviolet radiation from the sun, but does not let it out. As a result, the earth heats up, much like the inside of a closed car on a hot summer day. (This effect is called the greenhouse effect because this kind of heating also occurs in greenhouses.)

The Future of the Shore   Exactly how quickly earth's temperature will rise because of pollution is unknown. (A few scientists disagree over whether the temperature rise will occur at all.) But even a small rise in the earth's temperature—a few degrees—could kill off many animals and plants and cause a sea level rise that would flood low-lying coastal areas, including parts of Miami and Washington,

D.C. (Already, commuters in Charleston, South Carolina, check tide tables to determine what times of the day certain roads will be flooded.) Many seashore animal and plant communities are unlikely to adjust to the rising seas. Understanding how global climate changes and sea level rise affect the world's seashores are two of the greatest scientific challenges people face in the next century.

❀ 4 ❀
ROCKY SHORES

Pounded by waves, washed by rising and falling tides, and patrolled by hungry predators, the rocky shore offers its share of dangers. But even so, it is popular "real estate." For plants, rocky shores are good perches with lots of sunlight. Waves bring water and minerals. For animals, there's food—particles brought by waves or plants growing anchored on the rocks. Perhaps the biggest trouble for shore dwellers is finding space in such a popular habitat. And they've got to be adapted to hang on tight, or a wave might wash them away!

LIFE ON THE ROCKS

How do animals hang on to the shore? Methods vary. Barnacles cement themselves to rocks. Limpets hunker down in low shells, holding on with muscular feet. Mussels send out threads, stronger than steel, that anchor them to the shore. Sea stars get a grip on things with their hundreds of sucker feet. Holding on, however, is only half the battle, for on the rocky shore, other challenges arise as well.

Dangers on the Shore   Low tide, for instance, is a perilous time when intertidal animals—those that live between the low- and high-tide lines—are exposed to the air. In sum-

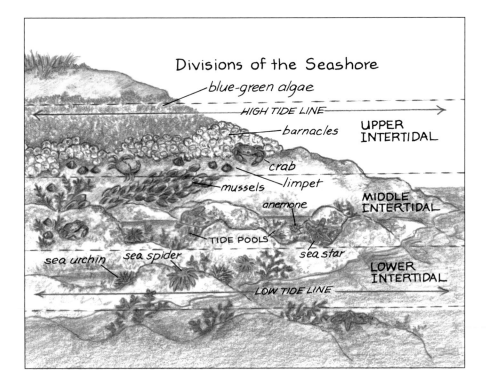

Divisions of the Seashore

blue-green algae

HIGH TIDE LINE

barnacles

UPPER INTERTIDAL

crab

mussels

limpet

anemone

MIDDLE INTERTIDAL

TIDE POOLS

sea urchin   sea spider

sea star

LOWER INTERTIDAL

LOW TIDE LINE

mer, the sun can overheat them, literally cooking their flesh. In winter, cold air may freeze them. Wind and heat can dry them out. Even rainfall, which is fresh water, can cause trouble for these saltwater animals. And then there are the predators: gulls, rats, raccoons, and people, who all wander the intertidal zone, searching for easy meals. Thick skins, spines, slimes, and other adaptations help intertidal animals combat predators and other dangers.

Watch the Zones   Animals and plants cluster along rocky shorelines in noticeable bands called zones. High up on the shore is dark, blue-green algae; below are white barnacles. Farther down are anemones, mussels, and even fish in tide pools at low tide. Closer to the water, where waves batter

32

the rocks, seaweed, anemones, and sea stars thrive. Zonation happens because environmental conditions vary up and down the shore. Close to the low-tide line, organisms are covered by water most of the day, exposed to powerful waves, and experience a constant temperature. High up on the beach, organisms rarely feel the waves and are touched only by the highest tides. Competition among animals, and danger from predators, also affect where animals live. And rock contours, crevices, shadows, and shelters can all change localized conditions for animals, varying the organisms that can be found in different zones.

The scientists here are measuring intertidal zonation—the distinct bands of life—on a California shoreline.

UPPER INTERTIDAL

In the upper intertidal zone, where tides rarely reach, living conditions can be harsh. Yet algae, limpets, and barnacles coat the shore, surviving even during low tide. Isopods and crabs scurry and skitter over the rocks to scavenge dead animals. Then they retreat to rock crevices where they can hide safely.

Got Those Blue-green Algae Blues   Blue-green algae coat the rocks and dominate the upper intertidal zone. These hardy, plantlike bacteria, also called cyanobacteria, can tolerate hot sun and cold winter winds. A gooey covering helps them reduce water loss. Lichens grow here, too, surviving the dryness by soaking up several times their weight in water when the tide is in. Limpets, like flattened domes, stick to the rocks, sealing water tightly in their shells. Both limpets and snails graze on blue-green algae, using their toothed tongues to scrape the slime off the rocks. These snails are even specially adapted to breathe air, unlike their lower zone, underwater counterparts.

The Barnacle Band   What creature stands on its head, catches food with its feet, and can travel without moving its legs? A barnacle. Below the band of blue-green algae, barnacles grow in a distinct white band. They can also live lower on the shore as well. These tiny relatives of shrimp live in volcano-shaped shells they build of calcium carbonate. Barnacles are filter feeders: when covered by the tide, they wave their feathery legs to gather tiny tidbits of food from the water. Most of what they get is plankton—tiny floating animals common throughout the ocean. But they also eat detritus—bits of dead plants, animal debris, and animal droppings. Just before the tide recedes, barnacles close two "doors" in the center of their bodies to prevent moisture

Gooseneck barnacles cling to rock on the shore of Washington State. Barnacles gather food from the water when the tide covers them and close up when the tide falls and they are exposed to air.

loss. Many that look dry and dead will "come to life" when immersed in water, pushing out their legs to feed.

Although they might seem like stay-at-homes, barnacles are actually world travelers. They spread to new places by releasing tiny larvae into the water. These larvae swim until they settle down, glue themselves to a surface, and develop a hard shell. Barnacles can be found on shells, the hulls of ships, and reportedly, even the feet of swimming penguins!

Stick-on Snails Limpets—those cone-shaped creatures that stick to rocks—are actually a kind of marine snail. Their stick-to-it-ive-ness is legendary: it can take 70 pounds (32 kilograms) of pull to get a 1-inch (2.5-centimeter) limpet off a rock. At night, limpets move slowly over the rocks and

This limpet is under attack by the sucking arms of a sea star.

graze on the algae growing there. Limpets are found in all three intertidal zones. Species vary in color from yellow to white to brown to green, and in texture from smooth to bumpy to strikingly ridged.

MIDDLE INTERTIDAL

Coated with seaweeds, barnacles, chitons, limpets, corals, sea stars, anemones, worms, and mussels, and patrolled by wandering crabs, the middle intertidal zone is chock-full of life. Its species are more diverse than those of the upper intertidal zone. And individuals are plentiful. This zone is wetter than the upper intertidal zone because it's more often covered by tides. Depressions in the rock also hold water during low tide, creating tide pools where aquatic creatures can survive until the tide rises again.

Awesome Anemones Sometimes striped, often brightly colored—in pink, green, red, or white—sea anemones look more like flowers than predators. But fish beware: these relatives of jellyfish have stingers. Stingers on anemones' tentacles are used for defense and to stun and capture fish, shrimp, and crabs for food. Anemones have strange and complex "family" lives. They can reproduce sexually, through eggs, but they can also literally split in order to re-

Anemones present a dazzling array of colors and shapes. Seen here are a giant green anemone (British Columbia, Canada), cherry anemones (California), and a northern red anemone (Arctic to Cape Cod; Alaska).

produce. One half of the anemone moves in one direction, and the other half goes the other way. Once split, each half can regenerate its missing parts to become a whole anemone! Such anemones are clones, meaning they're genetically identical to each other, and their 'parent' anemone. Sometimes anemones of the same species battle one another for space on the rocks, but clones won't harm each other. Somehow their fighting tentacles, called acrorphagi, don't harm tissue that has the same genetic identity.

Mussel Power The survival of mussels literally hangs by a thread—or many threads, to be more precise. Mussels begin life as tiny, free-swimming larvae. These larvae settle on rocks and crawl until they find a likely living space. Once settled, they send out tiny streams of fluid that harden to become tough, elastic strings called byssal threads. These strong-as-steel threads attach to the rocks by small, gluey plates. Many threads keep the mussel anchored strongly enough to withstand powerful waves. Among the forest of byssal threads and tightly packed mussels in the intertidal zone, other animals find shelter too. Gooseneck barnacles, worms, clams, shrimp, crabs, algae, and other creatures may live there.

LOWER INTERTIDAL

The lower intertidal zone is a riot of life. Seaweeds abound, in reds and greens. Anemones and colorful sea slugs called nudibranches feed. Sea urchins, sea stars, sea cucumbers, sea spiders, brittle stars, clams, mussels, and limpets stick to rocks. Unlike the upper and middle intertidal zones, the lowest intertidal zone has no dominant species that occurs in tremendous numbers. Rather, it's a place of amazing diversity—a remarkably large number of different plant and animal types.

Slick Advice   Take care if you're climbing over seaweed-covered rocks. Intertidal seaweeds have a slippery, slimy covering. The goo keeps seaweeds from losing water when the tide is low and they are exposed to the air. All of the world's 18,000 species of seaweed are algae, a primitive group of plants that includes the green, floating algae found in ponds. Seaweeds vary in color from green to purple to red to brown, and range in size from tiny specks of green algae to giant kelp that grows in underwater forests more than 100 feet (30 meters) tall. Rubbery, flexible tissues help seaweeds sway with waves and the tide. (The stiff, rigid stems and leaves of land plants would quickly break off or bruise under these conditions.) Gluey anchors, called holdfasts, stick seaweed to the shore. These plants don't have roots because they don't need them. They can absorb minerals and water directly from the ocean. Some seaweeds even have air-filled floats called bladders to keep them upright or near the surface, where sunlight is plentiful.

Underwater forests of kelp can be found off the coast of California (left). Air-filled floats keep the kelp upright (right).

· STARS OF THE SEA ·

When sea stars are in the neighborhood, other animals often make their escapes. Sea urchins and limpets crawl off. Clams leap up and flee. Pectens—animals that live in large brown triangular shells—swim out of reach. Why? Because sea stars are predators and they're legendary for their appetites. Sea stars eat so many shellfish—mussels and clams—that, in large numbers, they can hurt shellfish industries. In some cases, angry fishermen have cut up the sea stars to kill them and then thrown them back into the sea. Little did the fishermen realize that they'd just made the problem worse. Sea stars can regrow their arms, through a process called regeneration. One arm, and a bit of the center of the animal, can regrow into a whole sea star. In that way, one sea star could become five, or more!

Sea stars, or starfish as they are sometimes called, live in shallow seas, on shore close to the low-tide line, and in tidal pools. These star-shaped creatures usually have five arms, but some species have up to twenty-four. Sea stars come in a rainbow of colors—brown, red, pink, purple, orange, and green— and they can be up to 24 inches (61 centimeters) wide. They vary in appearance: brittle stars have central disks and very slender arms. Bat stars have arms connected by tissue, like a webbed foot. The sunflower star has up to twenty arms, making it look much like its flower namesake. (It starts with six arms and adds more as it grows older. Like other sea stars, it can shed arms as well, in defense.)

Like sea urchins and sand dollars, sea stars are echinoderms, or spiny-skinned creatures. (Speaking of spiny skin, the word *echinoderm* actually comes from Greek words meaning "hedgehog" and "skin.") When dead, sea stars' bodies are rigid. But when alive, they are quiet flexible. Loosely connected plates of calcium carbonate in their skin give them support but allow them to move. Sea stars can hug tight to a rock, wrap their arms around a mussel, and even use their arms to flip over if they get turned on their backs.

In a sea star, the jobs of the eyes, ears, and nose are done by the tips of the star's arms. Eyespots on each tip detect light. Small tentacles around each tip detect sound and "smell" chemicals in the water. To keep their surfaces clean, sea stars secrete a poisonous slime that discourages algae and small parasites from settling on their skin. They also have tiny pincers all over their tops, which constantly pull off unwanted barnacles, seaweeds, and other pests.

A sea star moves using its water-vascular system. This is a network of water-filled canals that runs throughout its body, all the way into its tiny sucker-ended feet, called tube feet. The sea star pushes sea water in and out of a tiny canal connected to each tube foot in order to operate the foot and its sucker end.

Sea stars have table manners that would shock any hostess. To eat a mussel, a sea star centers its mouth over the crack in the shell. It wraps two arms on one side of the shell and three on the other side. Then it pulls the shell slightly apart. (As you know if you've tried it, that's no easy job, but sea stars are very strong.) Next, the sea star pushes its stomach out through its mouth and pushes it inside the mussel's shell. Inside the mussel shell, the sea star's stomach releases chemicals that kill and digest the mussel. When done, the sea star pulls its stomach back into its body. Dinner's done!

Persistent Periwinkles Almost anywhere on the shore, from high above the water's edge to below the lowest tide, you can find periwinkles. This family of small, yellow, blue, black, or brown snails lives in spiral shells. They graze on algae, scraping it off rocks and seaweed with radulas—special tongues with about 3,500 tiny teeth. Periwinkles are so hardy they've been known to survive as long as two months without water. They've even survived being in a sea anemone's stomach! (The anemone spit the periwinkle out after about a day. Both animals appeared to be unharmed.) The key to a periwinkle's success is its operculum—a door in its shell that it can pull tight with its muscular foot. The door seals the shell to keep water inside and prevent the periwinkle from drying out during low tide. (By the way, if you get hungry, periwinkles have been eaten by humans for thousands of years. They're considered a delicacy in France.)

TIDE POOL STUDIES

In a tide pool, you can find countless creatures to study. (If you're not near a rocky coast, check your local aquarium. Many have supervised touch pools—artificial tide pools where you can pick up sea stars and other creatures and examine them.)

Exploring a tide pool

Materials you will need:
- Pencil
- Notebook
- Aquarium or pane of glass or rigid, see-through plastic

Tide Pool Tip: When you're working with aquatic creatures, keep them moist and don't let them overheat in direct sunlight. When you're done, return them to wherever you found them.

Here are some hands-on activities you can do to explore the tide pool world:

1. Pick up a sea star and gently place it on a pane of glass, plastic, or in an aquarium. Look at the sea star from underneath. Observe how its sucker feet move.

2. Try turning the sea star over to watch how it turns itself back upright.

3. Place a bit of seaweed on a sea star that is underwater. Observe what the sea star does with it.

4. Find some barnacles on a small object. Put the object in an aquarium or jar and fill it with ocean water. If they're live barnacles, their legs should emerge from the shell. Then you can watch them wave their legs in the water to gather particles of food.

5. Look at barnacles up and down the shore. Are they all the same size, color, and shape? Are ones that grow close to each other different from those that grow far apart? Write down your ideas and make drawings in your notebook.

6. Use a piece of seaweed, a small stick, or some other object—but not your fingers—to gently touch a sea urchin's spines. Observe how its spines move in response to the touch.

For more tide pool explorations, contact a seashore nature center or read *Discover Nature at the Seashore* by Elizabeth P. Lawlor (Stackpole, 1992).

TURF BATTLES ON THE SHORE

On rocky shorelines, competition for places to settle is understandably stiff. Most organisms have swimming or floating larvae that colonize bare spots when they appear. There's a subtle tug-of-war constantly taking place on occupied spots. Barnacles spread out, often covering low-growing algae. Large seaweeds prevent barnacles from settling down on rocks. Mussels muscle out both algae and barnacles, by simply settling down on top of them and attaching themselves with threads. For this reason, a mussel-covered shoreline is considered a "climax" stage in the rocky seashore's succession. (Succession is a sequence of animal and plant communities that replace one another over time.) Yet even with all this competition for space, bare spots on the shore still exist. The battering of the surf, and the predatory habits of snails and sea stars on mussels and barnacles, can create bare spots from year to year.

❀ 5 ❀
SANDY BEACHES

Many of the animals and plants you'll find on beaches aren't beach dwellers at all. Fish, jellyfish, whelks, and sea fans, for instance, are offshore creatures that are tossed onto the beach by waves. Few animal species can survive on sandy beaches, where sand moves daily, and the shore is often swept by storms. Also, food can be scarce, unlike on rocky shores, where a thick frosting of algae and living seaweed thrives. Not as many animal species live on sandy beaches as do on rocky coasts. But those remarkable species that are adapted to sandy beaches may occur in tremendous numbers.

BEACHES, TOP TO BOTTOM

If rocky beaches are places where animals hang on, sandy beaches are places where animals burrow in. Shifting sands make it impossible for animals to attach to the shore, so crabs, worms, and sand dollars dig down. Phytoplankton—tiny, floating plants—are brought by the tides. Waves also deposit dead marine animals and seaweed, which are scavenged by birds and crabs. Other animals dine on detritus washed in from nearby kelp forests, coral reefs, rivers, and ocean waters.

General Zones   Zones of life are less obvious on sandy beaches than on rocky shores. But they do exist, in a general way. On the upper, drier portions of beaches, look for amphipods and ghost crabs. Farther down, amphipods are joined by mole crabs and lugworms. Near the water, you'll find the most animals of all: polychaete worms, clams, and cockles abound. And when the tide is in, fish, shrimp, and other aquatic creatures may swim inshore to feed and spawn.

Hop to It   All over the sand, you'll find beach hoppers, or beach fleas. These crustaceans are 1 inch (25 millimeters) long and can hop 1 foot (30 centimeters) up in the air. But don't fear for your skin—these fleas won't feed on you. They're scavengers that dine on seaweed and other debris. If you use a flashlight at night on a California beach, you may see millions of beach hoppers hopping like insects in a field. Slightly smaller crustaceans such as amphipods and isopods skitter along the sand and may bang against your bare legs as they jump out of the way.

Ghosts and the Blues   When you find a crab shell on the beach, it doesn't mean a crab has died. As they grow, crabs must molt—shed their shells—and form new ones. (The "soft-shelled" crabs people eat aren't a special species. They're blue crabs that have been caught between molts, before their new shell has hardened.) Several crab species live on sandy beaches, and many more live offshore. Beach-dwelling ghost crabs—2 inches (5 centimeters) wide and chalky white or pale yellow—match their sandy backgrounds, which makes them even harder to see at night, when they're active. Another beach crab, the hermit crab, lives in the abandoned shells of snails. As hermit crabs grow, they must discard old shells and move into larger

TAKE THE MOLE CRAB CHALLENGE

The best place to find mole crabs is near the edge of the water. Look at the sand that is uncovered when the water pulls back between waves. The bubbling holes you'll see are likely to be mole crab burrows. Select a hole and dig down quickly with your hands or a shovel. Try to catch a crab before it escapes! It's a challenge to see one of these tiny crabs. They only extend their feathery antennae to gather food when waves are rushing over them. When the waves recede, the crabs burrow down, disappearing until the next wave comes.

ones. Some hermit crabs live in salt water and some live on land. So beware: a hermit crab you find on a beach may not make a good pet, like the ones sold in stores. It may be the underwater kind, which needs a saltwater home.

Between the Grains   Take a look at beach sand through a microscope. You'll find a strange miniature zooful of creatures. Spiny, spinning, skinny, tail-lashing organisms live in between sand grains, in a habitat called interstitial space. Bacteria by the millions coat the pitted faces of sand grains. Protozoans—one-celled creatures—slip in between the sand. As many as thirty different kinds of diatoms—microscopic, silica-shelled protozoans—can live wedged in the cracks on a single piece of sand. Yet each diatom is as beautiful as a snowflake and much more complex in its intricate silica shell. Other sand residents include meiofauna, or tiny, slender, multicelled creatures such as nematodes, roundworms, and shrimplike creatures. These animals, which dine on bacteria and diatoms, in turn become food for crabs and large worms, which sift through the sand to get at them.

MARVELOUS MEIOFAUNA

In this activity, you'll discover the life between sand grains.
Materials you will need:
- Scoop of sand
- Microscope
- One cup (250 ml) sea water
- Dropper
- Slides and cover slips
- Sketchbook
- Pencil

1. Examine a few sand grains under the microscope. Do you see any small animals?

2. Next, put a scoop of beach sand in a small cup of sea water. Some creatures should swim out of the sand. Use a dropper to pull up a drop of the water—no sand. Put the droplet on a slide and cover it with a cover slip.

3. Sketch the creatures you find.

Clam I Am   Jackknife, razor, bean, gaper, surf, or pismo, the names for clams are even more varied than the clams themselves. Clams are bivalves, meaning they have two shells connected by a hinge. Inside a clam shell is a soft body, called a mantle, and a thick muscle that holds the two shells closed. Clams are filter feeders. A clam's siphon pulls in water and the clam filters out plankton to eat. Along beaches, clams dig down into the sand. You may also find them tossing in the surf. Types vary. Tiny, rainbow-colored clams called coquinas are found in Atlantic surf. Gapers, or horse clams, have such big siphons and fleshy bodies that their shells cannot shut; instead they "gape" open, their flesh sticking out. Razor clams, long and thin like an old-fashioned barber's razor, can dig remarkably quickly, burying themselves within seven seconds. Pismo clams, white wedge-shaped clams up to 5 inches (12.7 centimeters) wide, were once so common on southern California beaches that horses pulled plows along the beach to turn them up from the sand for harvesting.

Digging for Dollars   Usually what you'll find of a sand dollar on a sandy beach is only its sun-bleached skeleton, called a test. When alive, sand dollars aren't white, but mainly brown, although some have a yellow, red, or purple tint. On the sand dollars' bottom and top are tiny spines, hairlike cilia, tube feet, and pincers that comb through sand for algae and other tidbits of food. Food is passed through grooves and transported to the sand dollar's mouth. The star pattern on the top of the sand dollar is made from holes where tiny tube feet stick out and help the sand dollar breathe. When danger approaches, sand dollars use their spines and tube feet to dig quickly down in the sand. De-

*You may be used to seeing the white skeletons of
sand dollars on the beach, or for sale to tourists (left).
Sand dollars look quite different when they are alive (right).*

spite their rigid shells, sand dollars are frequently eaten by fish such as cod, flounder, sheepshead, and haddock.

BIRDS AND THE BEACH BUFFET

On a sandy beach, you can watch birds dine and marvel at their feeding techniques. Gulls wander the tideline, scavenging food that has been tossed ashore. Sandpipers use the sensitive tips of their bills to poke, probe, and pry up prey. (Just by touching the sand, a sandpiper can feel the vibrations of worms and shrimps digging below!) Ruddy turnstones try another trick—turning over stones and shells to look for worms, crabs, and clams beneath. Sanderlings dash in as waves retreat, to get mole crabs before they dig down deep. Meanwhile, oystercatchers dine with style, inserting their red, blunt bills into oyster shells that are slightly ajar. The birds cut the muscles that hold the shells together, with a quick snip. Then they can open the shell and eat the meat within. Farther offshore, groups of pelicans dive down and scoop up fish in their 2-gallon (3.8-liter) pouches.

Eat Like a Bird   The expression "to eat like a bird" means you eat very little. But that's misleading: birds actually eat a lot. Sandpipers, for instance, must eat more than half their weight in food each day, just to keep their bodies going and not lose weight! Why are birds such heavy eaters? They have high body temperatures and fast metabolisms, so they burn up food quickly. Migratory birds need fuel not just for mating, nesting, and flying, but also for making their long migratory journeys.

World Travelers   Most shorebirds migrate. Lesser golden plovers, which can be seen in North America, spend their summers in the Arctic and their winters in southern South

America. In spring, plovers and other birds stop over at beaches to refuel for their long journeys. In Delaware Bay, these stopovers coincide with the spawning of horseshoe crabs. Hundreds or even thousands of horseshoe crabs crawl ashore to lay pale green eggs. Some eggs will hatch and grow into horseshoe crabs, but many are eaten by the birds, who need this rich "caviar" to survive.

Endangered Beach Bird Not only do birds feed on beaches, but some nest there as well. The piping plover lays its eggs right on the pebbles or sand. The eggs, and the young when they hatch, are so perfectly camouflaged that they are difficult to see. Since the 1950s, the population of piping plovers has declined drastically, so much so that they are now considered endangered. The disturbance of their habitat is a major factor in their decline. Dune buggies crush the birds' eggs. Foxes, dogs, cats, raccoons, and rats eat the eggs. (Many of these animals are attracted to the

*Shorebirds feast on horseshoe crab eggs
each spring in the area around Delaware Bay.*

A sign posted near a beach in Milford, Connecticut,
warns people away from an area where piping plovers nest.

beach by garbage left by beachgoers.) Also, piping plovers become alarmed if people or pets come too close. When this happens, the birds don't have time to forage for food and feed their young. As a result, some beaches are closed during part of the piping plover nesting season so these rare birds can raise their young in peace.

THE SAND DUNE SCENE

Like gigantic frozen waves, sand dunes border sandy beaches. They're formed from sand carried inland by wind. Sand drops down behind a rock, log, or grass clump, and gradually, a dune develops. Some sand dunes can build up to a height of 75 feet (22.9 meters), but 15 to 40 feet (4.6 to 12.2 meters) is more usual. The front of a sand dune—the side closest to the ocean—is usually gently sloped. Sand travels up the dune face, reaches the top, then drops down the sharply sloped back. Over time, many parallel rows of dunes can form, with valleys called swales in between. Dunes are most common on the Mid-Atlantic and Gulf Coasts, where barrier islands and sandy beaches are plentiful. But on the Pacific Coast, extensive dune fields occur on the coast of Washington and Oregon, and in California near Monterey Bay, Morro Bay, and a few other locales.

Dunes on the Move   Dunes are travelers. Marching forward at a rate of 3 to 16 feet (0.9 to 4.9 meters) per year, dunes can rapidly swallow roads, fill lakes, cover forests, and even bury houses. Grass can slow a dune's travels. Grass roots stabilize the dune, holding sand in place. But eventually, dunes will migrate anyway, as sand is blown by wind or carried forward by storm waves. Behind tall dunes, winds can scour out large low-lying spots called deflation plains. If a deflation plain is low enough, groundwater can seep in and form a spot where wetland plants can grow.

Dune Plants   Hot sun, cold nights, shifting sands, salt spray, strong winds, and nutrient-poor soils make dunes a difficult place for plants to grow. Yet American beach grass, sea oats, seaside spurge, woolly hudsonia, dusty miller, and seaside goldenrod thrive on the Atlantic Coast beach dunes. On the Pacific Coast, European beach grass, wild rye grass, seashore bluegrass, sandwort, beach pea, beach silver top, and beach morning glory survive. Like desert plants, dune plants are adapted to gather and retain what water they can. Taproots 6 or more feet (1.8 or more meters) deep help sea oats pull in water. (As the dune grows taller, burying the plant, the plant grows taller, too.) Leaves that are small and waxy or hairy prevent dune plants from losing much water to evaporation. But one thing these plants can't withstand is trampling, so pets and people should stay off dunes, to preserve these fragile plants.

Dig It! Dune Animals Hot, foot-burning sands and a scarcity of plants make dunes a harsh habitat. The main dune dwellers are insects: wasps, ants, grasshoppers, and beetles. But mice may live there, and foxes, raccoons, birds, and snakes visit dunes regularly. Dune insects and spiders escape the intense daytime heat by hiding out in cool, underground burrows and being active primarily at night. Many have amazing adaptations. Ant lions, for example, put the sand to work for them. To catch prey, they build sand pits with sloping sides. The sand pits are only a few inches wide. But insects stumble into the pit, fall down the

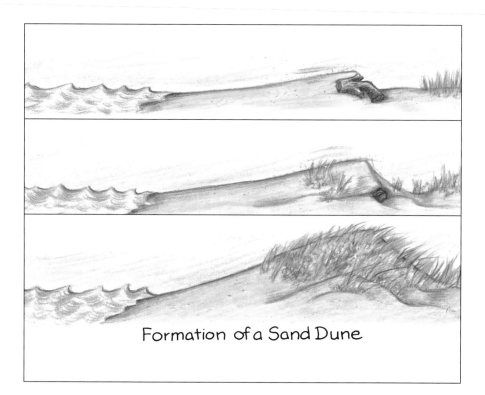

Formation of a Sand Dune

sloping sides, and slide into the jaws of a waiting ant lion below.

Coastal Contrasts   Dunes hold a startling array of life. Once grasses have established themselves, beach pea, verbena, and other small plants move in. Eventually, if soils are stable and water is available, trees such as pine, fir, spruce, and red cedar may grow.

Over time, people's activities affect how dunes change. South of San Francisco Bay, for instance, dune fields have been destroyed for housing developments. On Assateague and Chincoteague Islands, horses introduced by islanders decades ago have eaten back the beach grass, destabilizing the dunes. Ironically, on the West Coast, the problem in the Oregon dunes is too much beach grass! European beach grass, introduced around 1900, has changed the landscape drastically. It has stabilized the dunes, preventing them from moving, as they once did naturally. Now native plants and wildlife adapted to the moving dunes are suffering. In the future, the management of these and other nearby dune habitats and sandy beaches will require an intimate understanding of how these biomes work and how they vary from coast to coast.

PEOPLE AND SEASHORES

Whether for sun, fun, jobs, or the seashore's natural beauty, more people are moving to the coast each day. By the year 2000, an estimated 70 percent of the United States' population will live within 50 miles (81 kilometers) of a coast. (Half the population lives there already.) As people crowd closer and closer to the shore, conservation becomes more difficult. Coastal erosion and coastal pollution are two of the major challenges people must face.

THE BATTLE OF THE BEACHES

Even though beaches are dynamic, ever-changing places, people build on them as if they are not. And sand castles aren't the only structures that get washed away by the waves. Millions, sometimes billions, of dollars' worth of damage is done to coasts by waves and hurricanes each year. Towns are buried in sand as barrier islands slowly roll. Houses, lighthouses, and roads are washed away. Buildings once inland are left standing on stilts, lapped by ocean waves. And rising sea levels promise to make these problems worse.

Interfering With Natural Change   Beach houses, shops, and roads aren't just costly to build and doomed to be destroyed. They also interfere with coastal processes—the natural movement of barrier islands and beaches. Where human construction changes the beaches' movement, beaches often steepen, narrow, or wash away entirely. As the shape of the shoreline changes, waves often become stronger, and do more damage because the beach is not there to cushion their effects.

Making the Problem Worse To protect coastal developments, people often try to stop sand from eroding from a beach or filling an inlet. To do this, they build barriers. Long walls called jetties jut out into the ocean to keep sand from washing into inlets. Similar walls, called groins, stick out perpendicular to shore, to keep sand from one beach from flowing to the ones nearby. These structures may temporarily solve the problem in a local area, but they can prevent downshore beaches from receiving sand normally

A rock jetty off the shore of Ocean Grove, New Jersey, may slow erosion at this particular beach while causing a shortage of sand at other beaches farther down the shore.

carried by longshore currents. The jetties and groins in Ocean City, Maryland, are blocking southward sand flow to Assateague, a barrier island. Since their installation, erosion on Assateague has increased from 2 feet (61 centimeters) to 36 feet (11 meters) a year!

Walls of Futility   Another barrier that people build is a seawall. Seawalls line the shore to keep the shoreline in place and keep the sea out, protecting the buildings behind. But seawalls can eventually doom the beach that lies in front of them. Wave energy bounces off the wall and back toward the ocean, which causes the water to carry more of the beach sand out to sea. Over time, the beach becomes narrower and steeper, and eventually it disappears. The wall is then subject to even stronger ocean waves. (There's no longer a beach to help absorb the impact of the waves. And the shore has become steeper, which increases wave strength.) Along much of the New Jersey shore, beaches that people sunbathed on fifty years ago have washed away. All that's left are boardwalks and seawalls.

Pumping and Dumping   Yet another way that people battle coastal change is by physically moving sand. They dredge it out of channels to keep them clear: they dig it up from offshore and pump it onshore to form beaches. Miami Beach has already spent hundreds of millions of dollars pumping sand onto its beaches. This project has helped restore the beach, but the cost is very high—and a single storm could wash most of the pumped sand back offshore.

WATER POLLUTION WOES
What if you slipped on your bathing suit and traveled all the way to the beach, only to find it was closed? This very thing happens to countless people each year. In 1994,

beaches along the shores of the United States, including the Great Lakes, were closed or issued warnings that swimming was unsafe on 2,279 occasions. Water pollution is the reason. Swimming in polluted water can cause rashes, nausea, fevers, headaches, vomiting, pinkeye, and serious diseases such as hepatitis and giardiasis. Pollution is one of many environmental threats facing coastal regions today.

Slick and Disastrous   In some cases, water pollution is caused by obvious sources. In 1989, the *Exxon Valdez* wrecked in Prince William Sound, Alaska, spilling 11 million gallons (42 million liters) of oil that spread out over 10,000 square miles (25,900 square kilometers) of ocean, and 1,200 miles (1,940 kilometers) of shoreline. The oil killed an estimated 300,000 to 645,000 birds. Marine mammals—sea otters, whales, dolphins, seals—died in numbers ranging from 4,000 to 6,000. Fishing industries were crippled. Because it occurred in such a pristine area, along three national parks and three national wildlife refuges, the *Valdez* spill was probably the worst oil spill disaster ever, killing the greatest number of birds and marine mammals. Oil still soils parts of the beaches and coastline of Prince William Sound today.

Flush With Troubles   Most coastal water pollution comes not from major oil spills but from everyday sources. Sewage leaks from septic tanks and overflows from inadequate sewage systems. Boat engines leak oil, and boat toilets often flush their contents straight into the water. (In the Virgin Islands, snorkelers at some sailboat anchorages see toilet paper floating by!) During heavy rain, water from storm drains often overwhelms sewage treatment plants. At those times, raw sewage is often pumped straight into the ocean or bay.

• BUILDINGS OR BEACHES: WHOSE CHOICE IS IT? •

There's no question that coastal development interferes with the natural dynamics of coasts. Building on many coasts leads to narrower beaches or the disappearance of beaches altogether. Abandoning or relocating structures that are too close to the seashore is probably the only way to save the beaches in the long run. Yet it's difficult for people who have invested in beach properties to abandon them or not rebuild them after storms. After all, they are losing their money, their homes, or their businesses.

Property owners, however, aren't the only people who use and enjoy shorelines. Millions of other people visit and enjoy beaches during the day or stay in hotels located far back from the shore. Beaches are public property, after all. According to trade and visitors bureaus, coastal tourism is worth $1.3 billion in Alabama, $1.7 billion in Puerto Rico, $12.1 billion in New Jersey, $21.6 billion in Georgia, and $38 billion in California. Seashores are major attractions for entire coastal areas. Do these communities have the right to limit a property owner's building rights in order to protect the health of the beach for everyone else? The question is much debated in coastal communities all over North America.

What further complicates the issue is the fact that American taxpayers, even if they don't live near the coast, subsidize coastal development with their tax money. Federal disaster relief and low-cost federal flood insurance helps people rebuild along

Runaway Runoff Polluted runoff—polluted water that runs off the land into the water—is also a major problem. Water running over lawns, pavement, and other surfaces in developed areas picks up spilled oil, lawn fertilizers and

coasts after hurricanes and major storms. Yet hurricanes, major storms, and erosion are a fact of life along seashores. Money is poured into building houses in places where they'll likely be destroyed before long. In addition, federal, state, county, and city funds go to building seawalls and groins and to pumping more sand to maintain beaches. Everyone pays the cost for unwise coastal development. And scientists say it's a losing battle—the sea always wins.

Dr. Orrin Pilkey, a geologist who studies coasts, has been crusading for years for common-sense coastal planning. As he says, "You can have buildings or you can have beaches; you can't have them both." He recommends that buildings near beaches not be rebuilt after storms. The buildings should be moved much farther inland, instead. Structures near the shore, he says, must be accepted as temporary. Groins and seawalls should only be built if the community wants to sacrifice the beach to save the buildings. Replenishment should be used to "buy time" while planning to move buildings to safer spots.

In his fight to save seashores, Pilkey has found some success and some failure, too. Sweeping coastal building reform has not occurred. But in some cases, the use of federal money to rebuild on eroding coasts has been limited. North Carolina, South Carolina, and Maine have tightened their rules regarding coastal building. The seashore continues to be a battleground: not just between land and sea, but between people with different visions for the future of the shore.

pesticides, manure, industrial chemicals, and other pollutants. These pour into the ocean or rivers that lead to the ocean and move along shores. The sources of this kind of pollution, called nonpoint-source pollution, are difficult to pinpoint because the pollution comes from so many places. These and other kinds of pollution can devastate coastal areas, affecting both the wildlife and the people who live nearby.

PLASTIC POLLUTION

What's see-through; white, brown, or blue; and billows in the water? Jellyfish—*and* plastic bags. That's the problem. Sea turtles often mistake plastic bags for jellyfish—one of their favorite foods. Sea turtles eat the plastic bags and die. Plastic bags and other plastic garbage kills whales, dolphins, seals, sea lions, and sea turtles by blocking their digestive tracts. (A dead sperm whale that washed up on the North Carolina shore was found to have a gallon-size plastic milk bottle; a balloon-size plastic float; 35 feet (10.6 meters) of nylon rope; a garbage bag; and a piece of rubber 18 inches (46 centimeters) long, 6 inches (15 centimeters) wide, and 3 inches (7.5 centimeters) thick wedged in its digestive tract.) Marine mammals and birds also get tangled in plastics—in six-pack rings, discarded and in-use fishing nets, and other material. In the Gulf of Maine from 1991 to 1992, an estimated 900 to 2,400 harbor porpoises drowned in nets used to catch mackerel.

Garbage and other plastic pollution on seashores comes from both land and sea. For thousands of years, sailors have pitched their garbage overboard, assuming it would just "go away." It doesn't just go away, of course. Much of it is carried to beaches by ocean currents. Recognizing this problem, thirty-nine countries signed an international treaty in 1988 to prevent dumping of plastic in the ocean. That's just a start, but still more needs to be done to prevent plastic pollution from land-based sources worldwide.

OTHER ENVIRONMENTAL THREATS

Coastal development, sea level rise, water pollution, and plastic pollution aren't the only conservation threats to seashores. The following conservation issues arise as well:

- Dune buggies, dirt bikes, and other off-road vehicles can crush seashore animals, scare wildlife, and destroy vegetation. As a result, in National Seashores and in many other seashore communities, these activities are often restricted to limited areas.
- Dune grasses and other plants that help hold sand in place are trampled by beachgoers and easily killed off. Park officials often construct boardwalks and beach paths to reduce such damage.
- Baby sea turtles hatch at night and head toward the brightest light. Under natural conditions, that would be out at sea, where the moon shines on the water. But bright lights from coastal developments can confuse the turtles and cause them to head inland. To correct this problem, one Florida condominium association has reduced beachside lights by installing shields on outdoor lights and asking residents to turn off outdoor lights and close blinds and draperies at night during turtle nesting season.

WHAT'S BEING DONE TO CONSERVE SEASHORES

Efforts to conserve the seashore biome are varied and widespread. Every year in September, people from all over the world clean up coasts. In 1993, 224,058 volunteers—including many kids—from fifty-five countries cleaned up more than 5,000 miles (8,000 kilometers) of beach. What did they remove? *Five million pounds* (2.3 million kilograms) of trash, mostly plastic pieces, plastic caps, cigarette butts, plastic bags, and ropes. But they also collected a host of strange items including Barbie dolls, sinks, and even Christmas trees.

Oil-Spill Prevention   After the *Exxon Valdez* oil spill, people banded together to make sure such a tragedy would not happen again. New laws require double-hulled tankers, so in case of a wreck in which the outside hull of a tanker is pierced, the inner hull may help hold in the oil and keep it from spilling into the water. Other efforts, including new spill cleanup equipment, better handling of vessel traffic, and drug and alcohol testing for tanker pilots and crews, should all help ensure safer transport of oil.

Pollution Prevention   To reduce nonpoint-source pollution that flows into rivers and coastal waters, many people are trying to reduce their use of toxic products, fertilizers, and pesticides. Scout troops, schools, and church and community groups are stenciling storm drains with warnings telling people that the drains lead to streams or bays. And volunteers are working to educate their communities that what goes down these drains—and their kitchen sinks— can pollute rivers and coastal waters.

Turtle Helpers and More   At Canaveral National Seashore, volunteers patrol beaches in summer, helping to protect 3,000 to 4,000 sea turtle nests from raccoons, which eat the eggs. The volunteers wait until the sea turtles lay the eggs, and then they cover the nests with wire mesh that keeps raccoons out but lets the baby turtles leave after they hatch. These efforts have helped reduce the loss of nests and eggs from 95 percent to 20 percent!

The turtle program is only one of many to help wildlife in the seashore biome. From planting dune grasses, to clean-

*Human efforts have increased the survival rate
of baby sea turtles dramatically.*

ing up seashores, to monitoring nesting bird families,
seashore conservation efforts are as varied as seashores are.

THE FUTURE FOR SEASHORES
In the United States Congress in the 1990s, there's been an
ongoing battle between factions who want to weaken environmental laws, especially clean water laws, and those who
wish to maintain or strengthen them. At the time of this
writing, the outcome of the battle is unclear. But the result
is sure to drastically affect water quality along our coasts.

Helping Hands In the meantime, more and more people
are recognizing that clean water is not just important to

Drakes Bay, at Point Reyes National Seashore in California, is a beautiful example of a biome well worth conserving.

wildlife, but to people's livelihoods and coastal economies, as well. Whatever their reasons for concern about seashores, people are banding together to conserve this remarkable biome. But they could always use an extra hand! To find out how you can join in their efforts, read the next section.

RESOURCES AND WHAT
YOU CAN DO TO HELP

Here's what you can do to help ensure that seashores are conserved:

- Learn more by reading books and watching videos and television programs about seashores. Check your local library, bookstore, and video store for resources. Here are just a few of the books available for further reading:

The Audubon Society Nature Guides. Atlantic and Gulf Coasts by William H. Amos and Stephen H. Amos (Knopf, 1985).

The Audubon Society Nature Guides. Pacific Coast by Bayard H. McConnaughey and Evelyn McConnaughey (Knopf, 1985).

Discover Nature at the Seashore by Elizabeth P. Lawlor (Stackpole Books, 1992).

The Edge of the Sea by Rachel Carson (Houghton Mifflin, 1955).

Eyewitness Books: Seashore by Steve Parker (Knopf, 1989).

National Audubon Society Field Guide to North American Seashore Creatures by Norman Meinkoth (Knopf, 1981).

Peterson First Guide to Seashores by John Kricher (Houghton Mifflin, 1992).

The Seaside Naturalist by Deborah A. Coulombe (Fireside, 1984).

Tide Pools: The Bright World of the Rocky Shoreline by Diana Barnhart and Vicki Léon (Silver Burdett Press, 1995).

- For more information on conservation issues related to seashore, contact the following organizations:

American Littoral Society
Sandy Hook
Highlands, NJ 07732
Phone 1-908-291-0055

American Oceans Campaign
725 Arizona Avenue, Suite 102
Santa Monica, CA 90401
Phone 1-310-576-6162

Center for Marine Conservation
1725 DeSales Street NW
Washington, DC 20036
Phone 1-202-429-5609

Coast Alliance
215 Pennsylvania Avenue SE, 3rd Floor
Washington, DC 20003
1-202-429-9554

If you like the job these organizations are doing, consider becoming a member.

- Improve seashore habitat by participating in Coastal Cleanups each fall. For information on beach cleanups in your area, contact the Center for Marine Conservation at the address and phone number above. Or organize your own beach cleanup, any day of the year!

- Work to reduce your use of plastics that may end up in the marine environment. Plastic bags, ropes, bottles, and other items can kill wildlife. When you go to a store, bring cloth bags, old paper bags, or old plastic bags. Use these bags instead of getting new bags each trip. When you purchase an item, decide whether you really need a bag to carry it. Politely tell the check-out person if you don't need one. (Always carry the receipt for the item with you in case you need to prove you paid for it.) For cloth bags and other environmental products, contact the following company for a catalog:

Seventh Generation
Colchester, VT 05446-1672
Phone 1-800-456-1177

- Work with your family to reduce your use of toxic chemicals that can pollute coastal waters. Many products people use at home and in the yard—cleansers, paints, nail polishes, pesticides, and motor oils—contain toxic ingredients. These chemicals, when dumped on driveways, in streets, down storm drains, or down kitchen sinks, can end up in streams and rivers, which lead to coastal waters. Waste treatment plants usually cannot get all the toxic pollutants out of the water before they release it into streams, bays, and the ocean. Check your local library for information on household toxins and alternatives to those toxins. Call your local sanitation department and ask them about disposal programs for hazardous household waste in your area. You could also check the following publications for information:

Nontoxic, Natural, and Earthwise by Debra Lynn Dadd (Jeremy P. Tarcher, 1990).
Ranger Rick, April 1988 (a special Earth Day issue)

(For commercially prepared alternatives to toxic household products, contact Seventh Generation, listed on the previous page, or Real Goods, listed below.)

- Turn off lights, televisions, and other appliances when you are not using them. Reduce unnecessary car trips by walking, bicycling, taking buses, or combining trips. Saving oil and gas and the electricity, which may be made in power plants that burn oil and gas, helps prevent the need for the offshore oil drilling and oil transport that can lead to oil spills and other seashore pollution. Encourage your family to use energy-saving devices in your home. For more energy-saving tips, contact your local electric utility. For a catalog of energy-saving appliances and other environmental products, write or call:

Real Goods
966 Mazzoni Street
Ukiah, CA 95482-3471
Phone 1-800-762-7325

- Write letters to state and national government officials telling them you feel seashore conservation is important.

GLOSSARY

aquatic of, living in, or having to do with water

barrier islands islands close to and parallel to a mainland. These islands bear the brunt of ocean waves.

biome an area that has a certain kind of community of plants and animals. In the case of terrestrial biomes, but not in aquatic biomes, they have a certain climate as well.

byssal thread the threadlike material mussels produce to attach themselves to the seashore

current water that moves long distances and whose movement is unrelated to tides

dunes hills of sand sculpted by wind

ecotone a border between two biomes where the plants and animals of those biomes mix

greenhouse effect the warming of the earth's climate caused by the trapping of ultraviolet radiation from the sun by a layer of gases called greenhouse gases. Human-caused pollution is adding gases to this layer, increasing the natural greenhouse effect that may lead to global warming of the earth's climate.

groin   a wall built perpendicular to a beach to control the flow of sand

interstitial space   the space between grains of sand or other sediment

intertidal zone   the portion of the beach that is periodically covered by ocean water. This is the area between the high-tide and low-tide lines.

jetty   a structure built to protect a harbor entrance from waves, currents, or sand loss

longshore current   a current that runs parallel to the shoreline. This current is created by waves that are bounced back from the shoreline.

meiofauna   tiny animals that live between grains of sand and sediment

neap tide   tides that have the minimum difference between low and high tide. These tides occur at the first and third quarters of the moon.

nonpoint-source pollution   pollution whose origin is difficult to identify

rip current   a strong, narrow current that flows away from shore

runoff   water that runs off the land and into rivers, lakes, or the ocean

sea level rise   the rise in the average level of the ocean where it meets the shore. Sea level rise occurs when the earth's climate warms. Sea level has risen significantly in the last century.

seashore   the place where land and ocean meet

seawall   a wall built parallel to the shore to protect buildings and other developments behind it from ocean waves and tides

spring tide   the twice-monthly tides that have the greatest range from low to high tide. Spring tides occur at the full and new moons.

subtidal zone   the area below the low tide line. This zone is always covered by ocean water.

terrestrial   of, or having to do with, land

tide   periodic rise and fall in the ocean-water levels worldwide

undertow   the force swimmers feel from water that has hit the shore as breaking waves and is rushing away from the shore

wave   the rise and fall of surface water as energy passes through it

INDEX

PHOTO CREDITS